Prayers to Break Negative and Evil Soul Ties, Agreements and Covenants.

DANIEL C. OKPARA

Copyright © October 2016 by Daniel C. Okpara.

All Rights Reserved. Contents of this book may not be reproduced in any way or by any means without written consent of the publisher, with exception of brief excerpts in critical reviews and articles.

Published By:

Better Life Media.

BETTER LIFE WORLD OUTREACH CENTER.

Website: www.BetterLifeWorld.org

Email: info@betterlifeworld.org

This title and others are available for quantity discounts for sale promotions, gifts and evangelism. Visit our website or email us to get started.

Any scripture quotation in this book is taken from the King James Version or New International Version, except where stated. Used by permission.

All texts, calls, letters, testimonies and enquiries are welcome.

CONTENTS

FREE BONUS …5

Introduction…5

Facts About Soul Ties, Agreements, Vows, Pledges, and Covenants…8

Scriptures for Reflection and Confession…25

Prayers to Reverse Negative Effects of Unfulfilled Pledges and Promises….28

Prayers to Break Unholy Agreements and Covenants…33

Prayers to Break Soul Ties…39

Prayers for Deliverance from Undesirable, Destructive Habits and Strongholds…44

Prayers for Manifesting the Fruit of The Holy Spirit…51

Maintaining Your Victory…57

Other Books by the Same Author....65

Get in Touch...69

About the Author...70

FREE BONUS ...

Download These 4 Powerful Books Today for FREE... And Take Your Relationship With God to a New Level.

www.betterlifeworld.org/grow/

Introduction

This is a short and straightforward prayer manual with one goal in mind: *to help you pray and break any form of soul tie or ungodly agreement that you may have entered into in the past, knowingly or unknowingly.*

The Bible tells us not to yoke together with darkness because evil communication does **corrupt** good manners. Unfortunately, we think that **corruption** here is only in the change of attitude. No. The corruption that occurs as a result of yoking together with darkness can affect our spiritual lives, business, mind, health, and relationships negatively.

Soul ties and evil agreements are powerful demonic tools of oppressions against individuals. From time to time, we must prayerfully discern this bondage and address them with the name and Blood of Jesus Christ.

Facts About Soul Ties, Agreements, Vows, Pledges, and Covenants.

Be ye not unequally yoked together with unbelievers: for what fellowship hath righteousness with unrighteousness? and what communion hath light with darkness?

- 2 Corinthians 6:14

It is possible for someone to come under demonic attacks and oppression as a result of an unholy agreements, covenants, soul-ties or relationships. So let's look into breaking these unholy agreements, covenants and relationships that you may have entered into, knowingly or unknowingly, which is now a spiritual barrier to God's plans for your life.

SOUL TIES

Soul-ties are affectionate bonding between two souls. A kind of deep treasured relationship between two or more persons with a goal to work for each other's welfare and protection. It's so deep that each party in the relationship is naturally pulled by a force to remain loyal, never complain and to protect the interest of the other party.

After David had finished talking with Saul, Jonathan became one in spirit with David, and he loved him as himself.

Then Jonathan and David made a covenant, because he loved him as his own soul. **- 1 Sam 18:1, 3**

When a soul is tied to another soul for positive purposes it can bring about a great mutually beneficial good. But when one side seems to be on the receiving end, and yet cannot break free, it becomes an unholy soul tie.

There is a case that recently made a national headline a few months back. A man in his 30s secretly abducted a girl of 12-13 years old and continuously used the girl for his sexual gain. When the girl was found after several weeks, she initially refused to leave the man and said that she loved him.

Can you imagine that?

That is a clear case of negative soul tie. Whatever words or charms the man used to seduce the girl had gotten into her brain and soul to the extent she couldn't make sound judgments again.

Have you seen someone that is so involved with a person to the extent that even when it is evident that the person is just taking advantage of him or her, he still finds it difficult to leave this person? That's how a soul tie works.

Many times, soul ties start out as simple love relationships. It gets to a level where one party becomes the supplier of the love, and the ingredients of its service. Even when it's evident that he or she is being abused and hurt, he still can't find the courage to detach from the relationship. And even when forced to leave, he or she still can't move on wholeheartedly.

Soul ties are usually formed through sexual entanglements before marriage. That's why the Bible warns against sex before marriage because sex is not just what movies and friends say it is. It is a covenant. It is more spiritual than the physical enjoyment part of it.

Here are signs that you may be under a soul tie:

1. You are in an abusive relationship - physically, emotionally or spiritually – and you feel so attached to that person that you refuse to disconnect and set limits.

2. You are unable to move on wholeheartedly from a relationship you have left (maybe long ago). You continue to be obsessed with the other person (you can't get him or her out of your mind).

3. You continue to feel that this person is watching or monitoring you in anything you do. You feel that you cannot make a sound judgment without this person.

4. When you're having sex with someone else (your marriage partner), you can hardly keep yourself from visualizing this person.

5. You find yourself always comparing your present partner with this person. You always feel that your current partner is inferior to this person.

6. You may find yourself secretly stalking this person and still wanting to prevent him or her from having another relationship outside you.

7. You find yourself always defending this person; even when it's clear that you are hurt and

maltreated, you still feel that this person must be justified.

8. In some cases, you may find yourself unknowingly having same traits, moods and even sicknesses that this person is suffering.

9. You have an emotional reaction that is unpleasant when someone mentions their name or if you run into the other person unexpectedly.

Soul ties can pose a source of spiritual obstacles if not prayerfully dealt with.

NEGATIVE AGREEMENTS AND ALLIANCES.

Negative agreements can also be a

ground for satanic attacks against our lives. These may be just ignorant agreements of, "I will marry you," "You will marry me," agreements that a girl and a boy makes. They may go ahead to say things like, "If I don't marry you, let me not see good in life." Or even further to seal the agreement with blood or any simple token.

The disadvantage with these agreements is that spirits don't forget them. The boy or girl may forget and go on to live their lives, but the spirits that witnessed this **yoking together** will use it as a ground to afflict them so badly until this is discovered and brought to the light of the Blood of Jesus.

Another aspect of yoking together that can be a ground for the devil to build restrictions against a person is going into business with someone who has evil spirits and demonic influences, who may be under a spiritual judgment. Remember Jonah. He was under a spiritual judgment for disobedience and almost caused the people he was travelling with to sink until he was fished out.

We are not against business partnership at all. But we advise that before you go into any business alliance with someone, that you take some time to pray through and be sure you have an inner witness to go ahead with the business relationship.

UNFULFILLED VOWS AND PLEDGES

You also have these unfulfilled promises and vows here are and there that can be a ground for spiritual restrictions against a person. Solomon advised:

1 My son, if you have put up security for your neighbor, if you have shaken hands in pledge for a stranger,

2 you have been trapped by what you said, ensnared by the words of your mouth.

3 So do this, my son, to free yourself, since you have fallen into your neighbor's hands:

4 Go to the point of exhaustion and give your neighbor no rest! Allow no sleep to your eyes, no slumber to your eyelids.

5 Free yourself, like a gazelle from the hand of the hunter, like a bird from the snare of the fowler. – **Prov 6:1-5**

This scripture is very clear. It's possible

for you to have made promises and pledges that are now a ground for you to suffer some restrictions. If possible, go and unmake these promises and free yourself. That's what the Scripture is saying.

God is not happy when we make promises that we don't keep. Ecclesiastes 5:5 says that "It is better not to make a vow than to make one and not fulfill it."

Unfortunately, we are very guilty of this in charismatic circles. Many preachers try to entice people with sweet words and even outright lies and exaggerations to push them to make vows. And a lot of the time, most of these vows are not fulfilled, and we make more and more vows as the days go by.

Our prayers today will be addressing this folly. But there are two sides to it. First, if there are vows, pledges and promises you have made here and there, that you can point out; if you still intend to keep these promises, you must begin to work towards redeeming them sincerely; and afterwards, decide not to be pushed to make pledges and vows unnecessarily.

However, if you think you can't keep these promises any longer, then get back to the authority where you've done these pledges, call them and explain to them that you made some pledges sometime past, but that you can't fulfill them anymore. By so doing, you'll free yourself. And if they are not within your reach, we'll just pray and believe God to make a way somehow.

DIRECTION

Prayers to break negative soul ties, agreements and the effects of unfulfilled vows and pledges can be made anytime. However, we advise that you pray these prayers in the night. Remember, always start your prayers with worship and praise to God Almighty.

Scriptures for Reflection and Confession

1 Samuel 18:1 - And it came to pass, when he had made an end of speaking unto Saul, that the soul of Jonathan was knit with the soul of David, and Jonathan loved him as his own soul.

1 Corinthians 6:16,18 - What? know ye not that he which is joined to an harlot is one body? for two, saith he, shall be one flesh...

Flee fornication. Every sin that a man doeth is without the body; but he that committeth fornication sinneth against his own body.

Hebrews 4:12 - For the word of God is quick, and powerful, and sharper than any two edged sword, piercing even to the dividing asunder of soul and spirit, and of the joints and marrow, and is a discerner of the thoughts and intents of the heart.

1 Thessalonians 5:23 - And the very God of peace sanctify you wholly; and I pray God your whole spirit and soul and body be preserved blameless unto the coming of our Lord Jesus Christ.

Genesis 2:24 - Therefore shall a man leave his father and his mother, and shall cleave unto his wife: and they shall be   one   flesh.

Acts 4:32 - And the multitude of them that believed were of one heart and of one soul: neither said any of them that ought of the things which he possessed was his own; but they had all things common.

Prayers to Reverse Negative Effects of Unfulfilled Pledges and Promises.

1.

Heavenly Father, I come before You and confess my foolishness. Your Word says that those who don't fulfill their vows and pledges are fools and that You do not delight in them (Ecc. 5:4). How foolish have I been all this while!

LORD, I am really sorry for saying things and making commitments that I couldn't keep afterwards. Please forgive me and set me free from the restrictions from this attitude, in Jesus name.

2.

LORD, I ask You for grace and strength to obey Your Word henceforth. Help me by the Holy Spirit and keep me in constant reminder that I don't have to make promises and pledges to please men, but to obey You.

As I begin to work towards fulfilling my pledges from today, grant me wisdom and speedy breakthrough from this day forward, in Jesus name.

3.

Every demon raising accusations against me in the spirit due to my past errors, comments and unfulfilled pledges, I attack you right now with God's Word.

Romans 8: 1- 2 says, "Therefore, there is now no condemnation for those who are in Christ Jesus, because through Christ Jesus the law of the Spirit who gives life has set me free from the law of sin and death."

No demon has any ground to accuse me or bring an affliction against me. For I am now forgiven and set free by my Faith in Christ Jesus.

4.

I bind you foul spirits of hate and lies against my life and destiny and I cast you all into abyss, in Jesus name.

5.

With my mouth I confess that I am seated with Christ in the heavenly places, far above all principalities and powers.

I have been translated from the kingdom of darkness into the kingdom of Christ.

I am a bringer of light and a salter of lives and destinies.

I am moving from glory to glory even now and forever, in Jesus name.

Prayers to Break Unholy Agreements and Covenants

1.

Every negative agreement and covenant that I have entered into in the past, working against my life and destiny, by the Blood of Jesus Christ, I command you to break right now, in Jesus name.

2.

Every hidden evil covenant operating against my life and destiny, I renounce you, I reject you and I command you to break now in Jesus name.

3.

I nullify any evil covenant that I have been forced to enter through dream or my ignorance, in Jesus name.

4.

I nullify any covenant between me and the powers of the Water, the air, the moon, the sun, the rock, and the land, in the mighty name of Jesus Christ.

5.

Covenants made between me and any family idol and generational deities, be broken, in Jesus name.

6.

By the Blood of Jesus Christ, I break any covenant from my land of nativity affecting my glory and life, in Jesus name.

7.

Any evil covenant in the land or foundation of the house where I am living right now or I have ever lived before, affecting my life and destiny, be destroyed in Jesus name.

8.

Every evil law enforcement agency enforcing evil covenants in my life and family, be uprooted and destroyed by fire right now, in Jesus name.

9.

I plead the Blood of Jesus Christ over my spirit soul and body.

I plead the Blood of Jesus Christ over my life and destiny.

I plead the Blood of Jesus Christ over my business and career.

I plead the Blood of Jesus Christ over my house and environment.

I plead the Blood of Jesus Christ over my tongue and system

I plead the Blood of Jesus Christ. The Blood of Jesus Christ. The Blood of

Jesus Christ.

10.

By the Blood of Jesus Christ I announce that I am no longer involved in any other covenant. By the Blood of Jesus Christ, I am now in a new covenant of life, peace, divine health and prosperity with God the Father, God the Son and God the Holy Spirit, in Jesus name.

Prayers to Break Soul Ties

1.

Dear Heavenly Father, I confidently come before your throne of grace, covered in the Blood of Jesus Christ.

I ask You to disconnect me from any evil soul ties between myself and anyone else, created by any relationship, sexual or otherwise, known or unknown, in Jesus name.

2.

From today O LORD, I cut off all ungodly soul ties formed by any relationship, in Jesus name.

3.

Father according to YOUR Word, I present my body to You today as a living sacrifice, holy and pleasing to YOU.

From today, make me to offer true and proper worship acceptable to You at all times, in Jesus name.

4.

From today, I unyoke myself from every satanic yoke and distance myself from every unrighteous relationship, in Jesus name.

5.

O LORD, guide my footsteps to take the right path in my life journey.

Empower and guide me by the Holy Spirit to choose friends and relationships that will bring praise to Your Holy name, forever and ever, in

Jesus name.

6.

O LORD, as I encounter new individuals daily, my soul may become tangled with another causing me to idolize that individual and to lose sight of Your great plan and purpose for my life. I may even lose who I really am and who You created me to be.

LORD, in those moments of weakness, Let the Holy Spirit wake me up from slumber and remind me strongly who I am in Christ Jesus and help me to measure all friendships and relationships according to Your WORD, IN Jesus name.

7.

Thank You Heavenly Father for answering my prayers, in Jesus name.

Prayers for Deliverance from Undesirable, Destructive Habits and Strongholds

REFLECTION: Romans 12:1-2, Psalm 1:1-3, 2 Corinthians 10: 4-5.

1.

Almighty Father, I surrender my body to YOU this day. I hand over my thoughts to you and dedicate my mind, imagination and attitude to you henceforth, in Jesus name.

2.

O LORD, uproot out of my life every inner argument and unbelief contesting your Word in my life, in Jesus name.

3.

I hereby arrest every negative thought in me, resisting the move of the Holy Spirit.

I command these thoughts to wither by fire right now, in Jesus name.

4.

Every spiritual stronghold in my life working against the knowledge of God, I pull you down right now, in the name of Jesus Christ.

5.

I command all the false gods contesting for worship in my life, die by fire, in Jesus name.

6.

Every bad habit in my life, causing a

barrier between me and the power of God, O LORD, let your fire destroy them this moment, in Jesus name.

7.

From today LORD JESUS, plant in me an everlasting hatred for every work of the flesh as revealed in Your WORD.

I claim my freedom from every destructive habit.

You spirits of anger, lust, dishonesty, lying, spiritual laziness, pride, exaggeration, alcoholism, smoking, gossiping, and criticizing – by the blood of Jesus Christ, I declare that I am forever free from all of you.

I command you all to leave my life now and go into the abyss in Jesus name.

8.

O LORD my Father, whatever evil effect happening in my life, resulting from my characters, past mistakes, or addictions to negative thoughts, words and actions, LORD, please set free, in the name of Jesus Christ.

9.

Whatever curse and obstacle my wrong association and friendships have brought upon my life, O LORD, let them be destroyed today, in the name of Jesus Christ.

10.

Father, from now onwards, surround me with the right people; surround me with people who will challenge me towards a Godly and excellent life.

In Jesus name.

I commit myself never to walk in the counsel of the ungodly, nor stand in the way of sinners, nor dine with mockers.

Cause me by Your Spirit to find delight in seeking You and following Godly counsel.

Make me like a tree planted by the riverside that will bear fruit in all seasons.

In Jesus name.

Prayers for Manifesting the Fruit of The Holy Spirit

REFLECTION: - Galatians 5:22-23

1.

Heavenly Father,

Thank You for engrafting me in Christ Jesus by the Holy Spirit as a branch.

You designed me to bear fruits of righteousness, love, peace, joy, gentleness, self-control, goodness, patience, and kindness.

O LORD, I desire to bear these fruits in

my life henceforth,

In Jesus name.

2.

Dear Holy Spirit,

I desire to remain rooted in Christ, *bearing fruits that lead others to the light of God's love.*

I desire to walk in LOVE, *forgiving others at all times and gifting God's blessings in my life with others, just as God Loved and gave Jesus to die for us.*

I desire to walk in joy *every day of my life, thereby drawing from the well of salvation.*

Please remind and help me at all times to LOVE and be joyful as I live, in Jesus name.

3.

Dear Holy Spirit,

I desire to walk in peace *with myself and with others as a child of God.*

I desire to walk in patience*, for*

faith makes no haste.

I desire to walk in kindness*, thoughtfulness and compassion for others just as Christ was compassionate at all times.*

*Provide me with daily assistance to bear these fruits of **peace, patience** and **kindness** in abundance, so that Jesus will be glorified in my life every day, in Jesus name.*

4.

Dear Holy Spirit,

I desire to bear the fruit of Goodness, *so that I may lead others to Jesus Christ.*

I desire to be faithful *at all times with whatever God blesses me with, so that I may stand before God in the end and receive the rewards of faithfulness.*

I desire to be gentle *with myself and others, in thoughts, words and actions, so that I may be an instrument of encouragement and uplifting to others and not discouragement.*

I desire to walk in Self-control *in food, dressing, and in everything so* *that I could win the race set before me and not be a cast away after preaching to others.*

I call upon You to empower me every day to bear these fruits as I live, serve God and relate with others.

In Jesus name I pray. Amen.

Maintaining Your Victory

"When the unclean spirit has gone out of a person, it passes through waterless places seeking rest, but finds none.

Then it says, 'I will return to my house from which I came.' And when it comes, it finds the house empty, swept, and put in order.

Then it goes and brings with it seven other spirits more evil than itself, and they enter and dwell there, and the last state of that person is worse than the first. So also will it be with this evil generation." – **Matt. 12:43-45**

Jesus is simply saying here that there is

a probability that one gets delivered from sickness, curses and evil spirit attacks and the problems come back again and the situation becomes worse than it was in the beginning.

But it doesn't have to be so.

The Word of God gives us an idea of how we can keep our deliverance and victory permanent.

---

1. DO NOT KEEP YOUR SPIRIT EMPTY.

From Jesus' statement above, it's obvious that if you leave your spirit empty, you might get attacked with a worse situation.

Consequently, it's important to fill your mind with positive thoughts and vibrations. Fill your mind with God's Word on a daily basis.

"Keep this Book of the Law always on your lips; meditate on it day and night, so that you may be careful to do everything written in it. Then you will be prosperous and successful. - ***Joshua 1:8"***

Work out a system to read the Bible daily, one or two chapters a day and your spirit will have content that will resist the enemy at all times.

---

2. SERVE THE LORD.

"So you shall serve the LORD your God, and He will bless your bread and your water. And I will take sickness away from the midst of you. No one shall suffer miscarriage or be barren in your land; I will fulfill the number of your days." - **Exodus 23:25-26:**

Find a place in God's kingdom and do His work. Join in sharing tracts, the prayer team, the ushering department… just get busy for the LORD, and no enemy will have grounds over your life

3. EXERCISE YOUR FAITH.

It is possible that you experience some form of attack, temptation, and setback in your life, from time to time. That doesn't necessarily mean that you are not delivered.

It's important for you to believe that you have been delivered and confess your deliverance, and stop running to and fro looking for other types of prayers for deliverance any more. Remember what the Bible says:

"Now faith is the assurance (title deed, confirmation) of things hoped for (divinely guaranteed), and the evidence of things not seen [the conviction of their reality—faith comprehends as fact what cannot be experienced by the physical senses]. 2 For by this [kind of] faith the [a]men of old gained [divine] approval - **Hebrews 11:1(AMP).**

---

4. SHARE YOUR TESTIMONY.

When you share your story with others, your blessings become permanent.

Jesus told the healed man…

"Return to your home, and declare how much God has done for you." And he went away, proclaiming throughout the whole city how much Jesus had done for him - **Luke 8:39 (ESV)**

---

5. LEARN TO MAINTAIN A POSITIVE OUTLOOK ABOUT LIFE AND KEEP SPEAKING POSITIVE THINGS ABOUT YOUR LIFE.

Proverbs 18:21 - Death and life [are] in the power of the tongue: and they that love it shall eat the fruit thereof.

1 Peter 3:10 - For he that will love life, and see good days, let him refrain his tongue from evil, and his lips that they speak no guile:

Ephesians 4:29 - Let no corrupt communication proceed out of your mouth, but that which is good to the use of edifying, that it may minister grace unto the hearers.

God bless you.

Other Books by the Same Author.

1. Prayer Retreat: 21 Days Devotional With 500 Prayers & Declarations to Destroy Stubborn Demonic Problems.

2. HEALING PRAYERS & CONFESSIONS: Daily Meditations, Prayers and Declarations for Total Healing and Divine Health.

3. 200 Violent Prayers for Deliverance, Healing and Financial Breakthrough.

4. Hearing God's Voice in Painful Moments: Meditations, Prayers and Declarations to Bring Comfort, Strength, and Healing When Grieving the Loss of Someone You Love.

5 . Healing Prayers: Prophetic Prayers that Brings Healing

6. Healing WORDS: Daily Confessions & Declarations to Activate Your Healing.

7. Prayers That Break Curses and Spells and Release Favors and Breakthroughs.

8. 120 Powerful Night Prayers That Will Change Your Life Forever.

9. How to Pray for Your Children Everyday: + Prayers & Prophetic Declarations to Use and Pray for Your Children

10. How to Pray for Your Family

11. Daily Prayer Guide: A Practical Guide to Developing a Powerful Personal Prayer Life

12. Make Him Respect You: 31 Very Important Relationship Advice for Women to Make their Men Respect Them.

13. How to Cast Out Demons from Your Home, Office & Property: Prayers to Cleanse Your Home, Office, Land & Property from Demonic Attacks

14. Praying Through the Book of Psalms: Selected Psalms, Prayers & Declarations for Every Situation.

15. STUDENTS' PRAYER BOOK: Motivation & Guide for Students Preparing to Write Exams -

Plus 10-Day Prayers for Wisdom, Favor, Protection & Success

16. How to Pray and Receive Financial Miracle: Powerful Prayers for Financial Miracles, Business and Career Breakthrough

17. Powerful Prayers to Destroy Witchcraft Attacks.

18. Deliverance from Marine Spirits: Prayers to Overcome Marine Spirits – Spirit Husbands and Spirit Wives – Permanently

19. Deliverance From Python Spirit: Prayers to Defeat the Python Spirit – Spirit of Lies, Deceptions, and Oppression.

20. Anger Management God's Way: Controlling Your Emotions, Getting Healed of Hurts & Responding to Offenses …Plus: Daily Prayers to Overcome Bad Anger Permanently

21. How God Speaks to You: Simple Guide to Hearing the Voice of God Clearly & Following His Direction for Your Life

22. Deliverance of the Mind: Prayers to Deal With Mind Control, Fear, Anxiety, Depression, Anger

and Other Negative Emotions

23. Most Commonly Asked Questions About Demons: How to Cast Out Demons and, Obtain Deliverance.

24. Praying the Promises of God for Daily Blessings and Breakthrough.

25. When God Is Silent! What to Do When Prayer Seems Unanswered or Delayed

26. I SHALL NOT DIE: Prayers to Overcome the Spirit and Fear of Death.

27. Praise Warfare: Overcoming Your Fears, Worries & Battles with the Power of Praise

See all at:

www.amazon.com/author/danielokpara

Get in Touch

We love testimonies. We love to hear what God is doing around the world as people draw close to Him in prayer. Please share your story with us.

Also, please consider giving this book a review on Amazon and checking out our other titles at: amazon.com/author/danielokpara .

Kindly do checkout our website at www.BetterLifeWorld.org, and send us your prayer request. As we join faith with you, God's power will be made manifest in your life.

About the Author

Daniel Chika Okpara is the author of over 50 life changing books on business, prayer, relationship and victorious living.

He is the president of Better Life World Outreach Centre -www.betterlifeworld.org - a non-denominational evangelism ministry committed to global prayer revival and evangelism.

He holds a Master's Degree in and is married to his lovely wife, Doris, his prayer warrior, best friend and biggest support in life. They are blessed with two lovely children.

NOTES

Made in the USA
Lexington, KY
05 April 2019